Schaum Making Music Method

Level One

By John W. Schaum
Revised and Edited by Wesley Schaum

FOREWORD

The Schaum *Making Music Method* uses the proven middle-C approach integrated with ear, eye and finger training. This edition is the product of many years of teaching experience and continuing evaluation. Many careful refinements enhance the original pedagogic concepts.

Preparatory drills *(Finger Workouts* and *Rhythm Sections)* are used to introduce and reinforce new rhythms and technic configurations. **Duet accompaniments** provide opportunities for rhythmic training and ensemble experience.

Independence of the hands is developed through cross-hand work. **Scale** construction and playing are emphasized. **Transposition** is taught by using different hand positions.

The music notation gives the student a **visual image of the rhythm** by making the measures in each piece of equal width.

Self-help is encouraged by the inclusion of *Reference Pages* and a *Music Dictionary* in the book. The student can sound out pronunciations of musical terms by using the phonetic syllables provided.

The majority of music is *original*, composed by John W. Schaum. There are also transcriptions of folk songs and themes from outstanding educational keyboard composers.

The Schaum *Making Music Method* consists of *six books*, from Primer Level through Level 5

Schaum Publications, Inc.

CONTENTS

Schaum's Curriculum for Musicianship Development

Student musicianship is developed by a balanced curriculum that includes:
- Note Reading and Music Theory
- Finger Strength and Dexterity
- Music Appreciation and Repertoire Development
- Rhythmic Training and Ensemble Experience

Schaum's 2-Way Flash Cards

Unique features:
- May be used right-side up and upside down.
- Each column has a different key signature.
- Answers are printed on the back.

Preparation and storage:

1. The flash cards may be made more durable by covering the entire page with *clear contact paper*, both front and back.

2. Cut apart on the dotted lines.

3. After cutting, keep the flash cards in an *envelope* taped to the back inside cover of this book.

Recommendations for use:

- As each key signature occurs in the book, the matching column of flash cards may be used. For example, use the F major flash cards with "Pancakes" on page 7. Use G major flash cards with "Chipmunks" on page 9, etc.

- Flash cards should be *reviewed* frequently.

- To encourage speed, the student may be timed with a watch. Keep track of the time and date in a notebook.

- May also be *used at home* with help from parents.

The answers are printed on the back of each flash card for the convenience of parents and teacher.

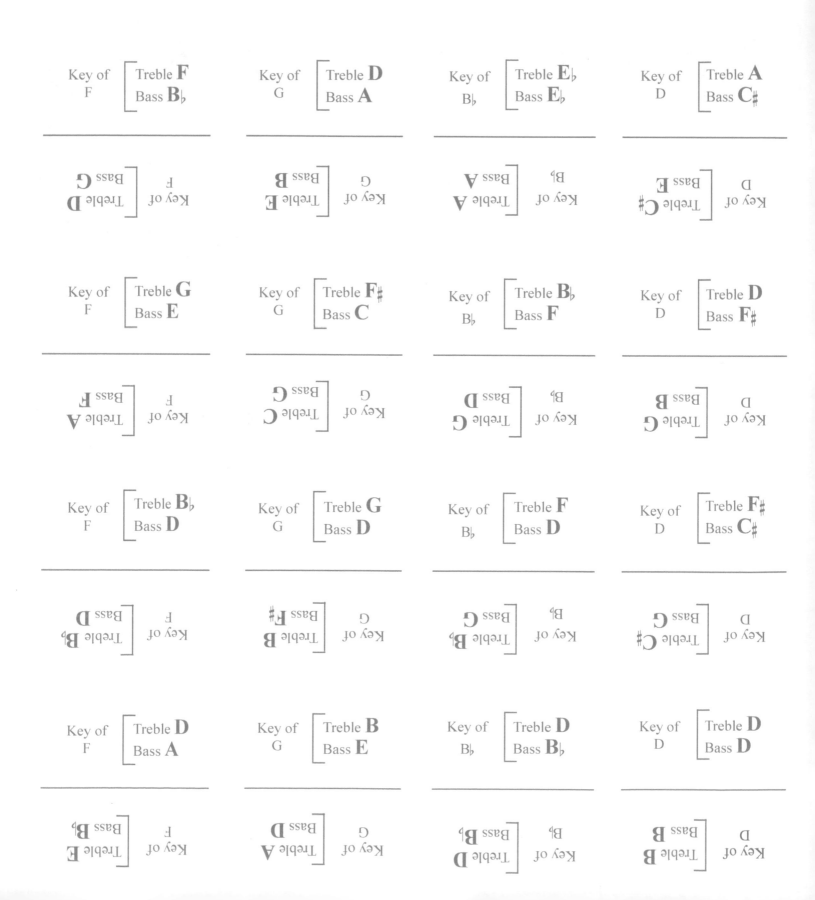

Right Hand Position

Left Hand Position

G A B C D E F G

"SEE-MORE" the Note Watcher says: look for the **TIE** in the first and third lines of music. (See footnote.)

Melodyland

This is the land of mel - o - dy, where

p

Tie*

mu - sic grows on ev - 'ry tree. The tunes are in a

f

mag - ic key, En - chant - ed you will sure - ly be.

Tie*

Accompaniment (stem up = RH – stem down = LH):

*A *tie* is a curved line that connects two notes *in the same line or space* that are *next to each other*. The second note is *not played*, but should be held down by the finger to form one continuous sound with the first note.

6

Finger Workout*

Play this exercise five times daily to help strengthen your fingers.

The **Repeat Sign** means go back to the beginning and play again.

The Syrup Tree

French Folk Song

Tap, tap, tap! | Ma - ple sap, | Drip - ping in - to | syr - up buck - ets.

Tap, tap, tap! | Ma - ple sap, | It's the first sure | sign of spring.

Accompaniment

The "Syrup Tree" refers to the sugar maple. Early in the month of March, syrup buckets are attached to hundreds of thousands of trees in Maine, Massachusetts, New Hampshire and Vermont. Sap from the trees drips into the buckets. The sap is processed in big vats to make maple syrup, which is used on pancakes.

*Teacher's Note: The *Finger Workout* is a **technic preparatory** drill. The notes should be played with a firm legato touch. The rhythm patterns in the *Finger Workout* prepare the student for the patterns in this piece.

SIMILAR PHRASES

Music is made up of phrases. This piece consists of 4-note phrases and 5-note phrases.

All 4-note phrases have the *same notes* except the measure with the F# in the bottom line.

Each 5-note phrase has the *same rhythm* pattern.

Recognizing similar phrases will help make reading and memorizing music easier.

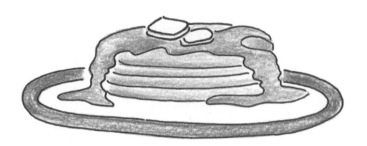

Key of F Major
Play every "B" flat as a pancake!

Pancakes

Accompaniment

Teacher's Note: F major *flash cards* should be cut apart and used as directed (see page 3).

8

Finger Workout

Play this exercise five times daily to help strengthen your fingers.

*phrase mark

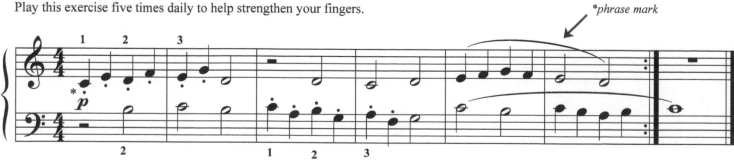

Catch a Falling Snowflake

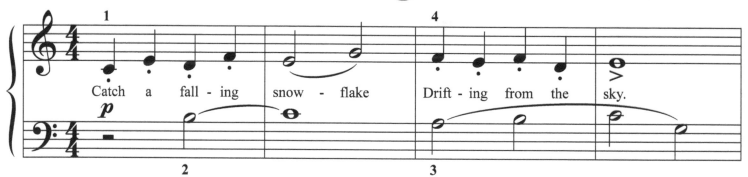

Catch a fall - ing snow - flake   Drift - ing from the sky.

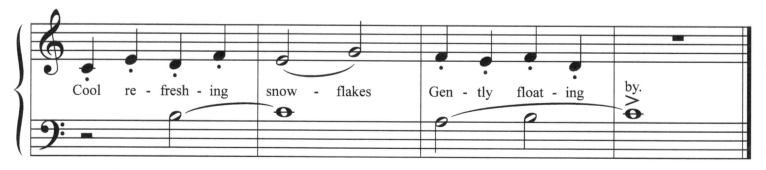

Cool re - fresh - ing snow - flakes   Gen - tly float - ing by.

Accompaniment (*Play one octave higher*)

*Notes with dots are to be played *staccato*. Notes connected by a *phrase mark* are to be played *legato*. Look up the definitions of *legato*, *phrase mark* and *staccato* in the Music Dictionary on pages 46-47.

 Find the two *accent* marks (>) in this piece. Look up *accent* in the Dictionary on page 46.

Teacher's Note: Schaum's **Theory Workbook, Level 1** (catalog #02-81) is recommended as a supplement.

DISSONANCE

Dissonance is a harsh, disagreeable sound sometimes found in music.

A *dissonance* occurs on the word "croak," at the end of the 1st line of music, and on the word "speech," at the end of the 3rd line of music.

These dissonances are intended to humorously suggest the voices of the frog and chipmunk.

Chipmunks

C = Common Time (4/4)

f One squeak - y chip - munk Hears a bull - frog croak. The *p*

New note: C#

oth - er squeak - y chip - munk Quick - ly climbs an oak.

f One squeak - y chip - munk Makes a nois - y speech. The *p*

oth - er squeak - y chip - munk Scam - pers out of reach.

Accompaniment

Teacher's Note: G major *flash cards* should be cut apart and used as directed (see page 3).

Over the Rainbow

Right hand *Intervals

Third   *Second*

Sun - shine through rain makes a col - or - ful rain - bow. Sto - ries are told that you'll find wealth and

*An **interval** is the distance in sound between one note and another.
The interval number is the *same* as the number of alphabet letters.
In the treble staff of this piece, the right hand plays only these two intervals:

E to G is a **3rd** because the distance is **three** alphabet letters (E-F-G).

F to G is a **2nd** because the distance is **two** alphabet letters (F-G).

Play all the *3rds* – how many are there? _____   Play all the *2nds* – how many are there? _____

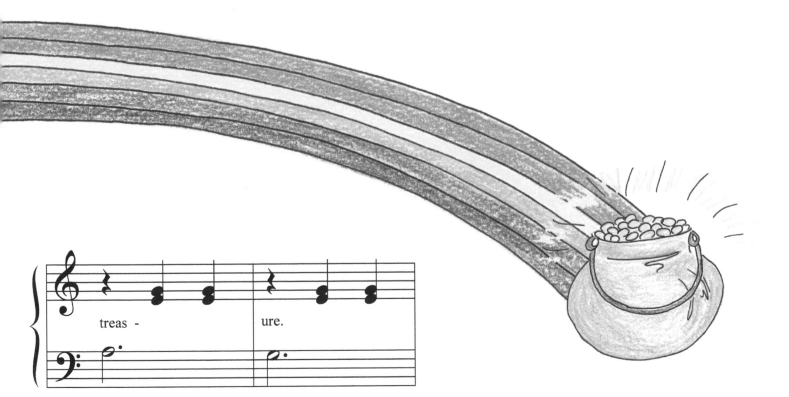

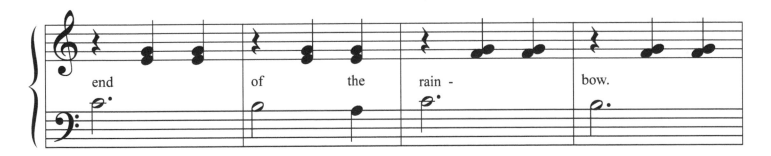

treas -   ure.

_p_ **2** Fol -   low   the   trail   to   the

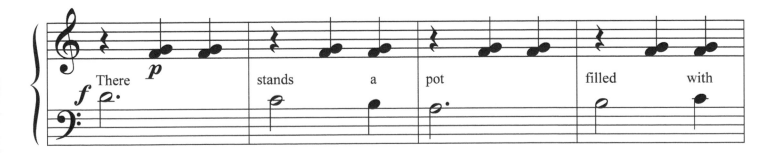

end   of   the   rain -   bow.

There _p_   stands   a   pot   filled   with

_f_

gold   for   your   pleas -   ure.

(Notice the ♯ eye)

Sharp-eye the Fox

This piece is played entirely on the black keys. Check the keyboard chart above.

Sharp - eye   is   a   clev - er   fox,   Hunt - ing   day   or   night.

Be   like   Sharp - eye,   watch   each   sharp,   Go   up   one   key   to   the   right.

This accompaniment may also be used for page 13.

EACH BLACK KEY
HAS TWO NAMES

C♯ and D♭ are two names for the same black key. Another black key is named either F♯ or G♭.

The keyboard diagram at the top of this page shows the *sharp* key names and the notes on the staff. The other diagram at the top of page 13 shows the *flat* key names and notes for the *same black keys*.

The melody for the pieces on pages 12 and 13 *sounds the same*, but is *written differently*.
In "Sharp-eye the Fox" all of the notes are *sharps*. In "Flat-foot the Duck" all of the notes are *flats*.

In our language, there are *words* that *sound the same* but are *spelled differently*, such as:
RIGHT and WRITE – ONE and WON.

Finger Workout

This exercise is played entirely on the black keys. See the keyboard chart below.
Play it five times each day as a warmup.

(Notice the ♭ feet)

Flat-foot the Duck

This piece is played entirely on the black keys. Check the keyboard chart above.

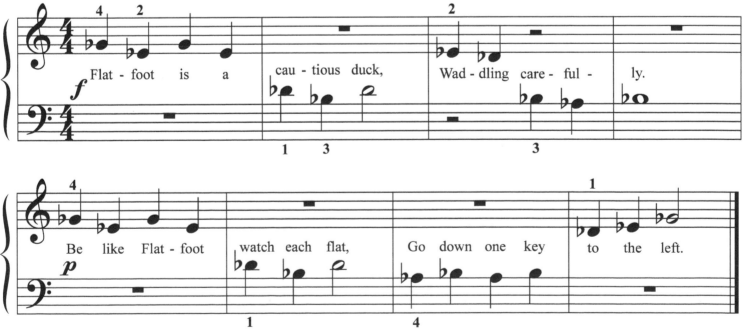

Flat - foot   is   a   cau - tious duck,   Wad - dling care - ful - ly.

Be   like   Flat - foot   watch each flat,   Go   down   one   key   to   the   left.

Teacher's Note: The melodies on pages 12 and 13 may be TRANSPOSED one half step by playing them entirely on the WHITE KEYS. In "Sharp-eye the Fox," the student should pretend that there are *no sharps*, as the piece is played.
In "Flat-foot the Duck," pretend that there are *no flats*.

14

Rhythm Section (Preparatory)

Count aloud, 1 – 2, to each measure and clap hands, one clap with each note. Make a little accent on all of the ONE counts. This is the rhythm pattern for "Cuckoo and the Parakeet."

Left Hand *Bass C* position

Cuckoo and the Parakeet

Two Counts per measure

"Cuck - oo, Cuck - oo, Cuck - oo, Cuck - oo." The

cuck - oo tells the par - a - keet. "Cuck - oo, Cuck - oo, Cuck -

oo, Cuck - oo." "You're cuck - oo," says the par - a - keet.

Accompaniment *(play one octave higher)*

Rhythm Section (Preparatory)

Count aloud, 1 – 2 – 3 – 4, to each measure and clap hands, one clap with each note. Make a little accent on all of the ONE counts.

Ponies

Place left hand in *Bass C position* (see page 14).

French Folk Tune

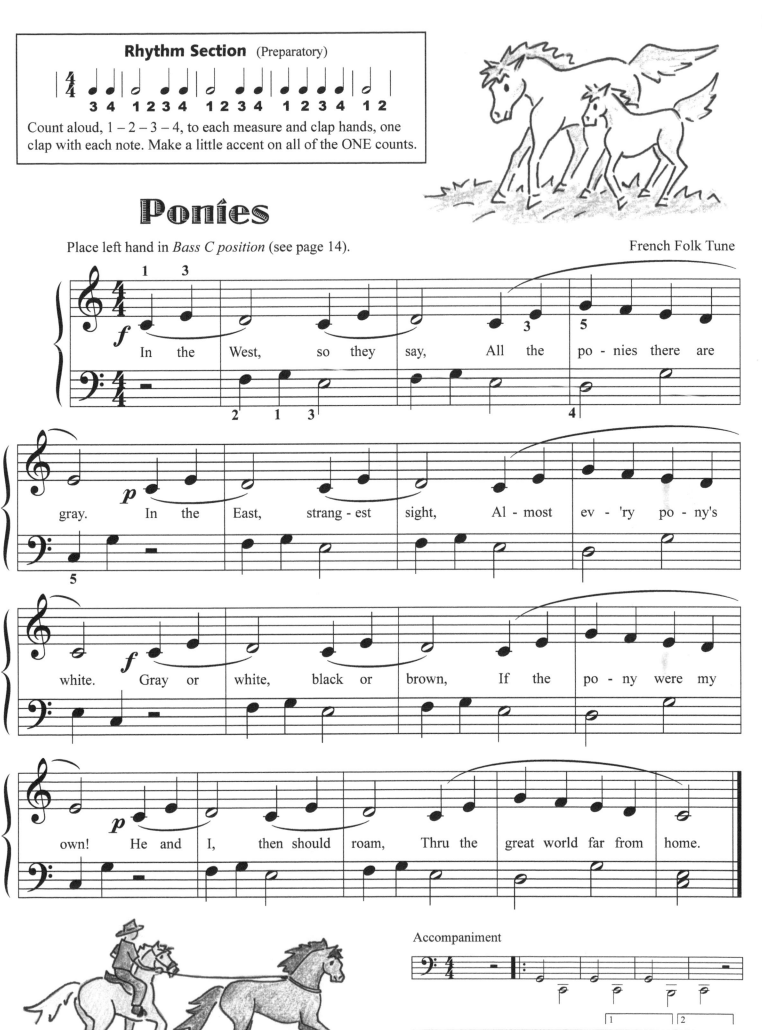

In the West, so they say, All the po - nies there are gray. In the East, strang - est sight, Al - most ev - 'ry po - ny's white. Gray or white, black or brown, If the po - ny were my own! He and I, then should roam, Thru the great world far from home.

Accompaniment

Benjamin Franklin

Place left hand in *Bass C position* (see page 14).

Allegretto *(medium fast)*

Folk Melody

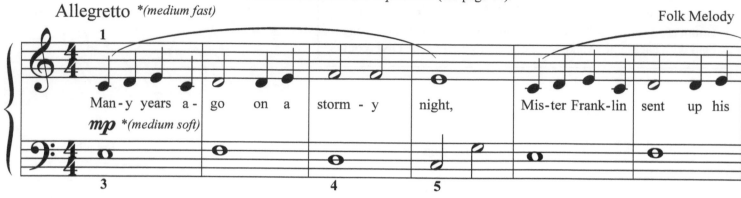

Man-y years a - go on a storm-y night,   Mis-ter Frank-lin sent up his

mp *(medium soft)*

fa - mous   kite.   Light-ning pro-duced e-lec-tric-i-ty,

f

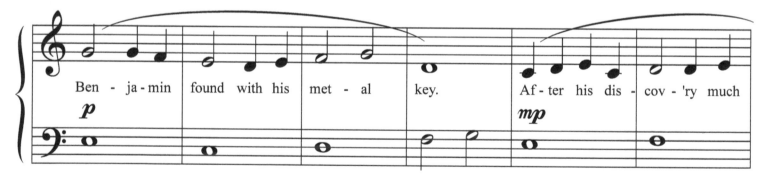

Ben-ja-min found with his met-al key.   Af-ter his dis-cov-'ry much

p   *mp*

prog-ress came,   And the world has nev-er been quite the same.

f   *rit.* *(gradually — — — slower — — — — —)*

Accompaniment

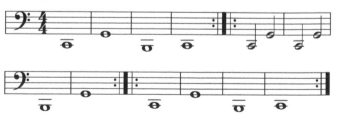

*Pronunciations and definitions of musical words may be found in the **Music Dictionary** on pages 46-47.

Rhythm Section (Preparatory)

Count aloud, 1 – 2 – 3, to each measure and clap hands, one clap with each note. Make a little accent on all of the ONE counts.

Star Gazing

Moderato *(Moderate speed)*

p Star gaz-ing af-ter dark on a night when the sky is clear.

legato (smooth and connected)

Big Dip-per can be seen if it is the right sea-son of the year.

mp

Some-times a shoot-ing star flash-es bright with a streak of light.

f

As-tro-nauts are mak-ing space flights that take them up to the moon.

rit.

CROSS-HAND PLAYING
Each of these three pieces uses the *same notes*. In the first piece, the hands are in the normal position. However, in the last two pieces, the hands are *crossed*. Watch for different positions of the *clefs*.

The Expressway

Over the Bridge

Cross the Right hand **OVER** the Left hand.
(Right hand plays notes in the Bass staff)

(Left hand plays notes in the Treble staff)

Under the Bridge

Cross the Right hand **UNDER** the Left hand.
(Right hand plays notes in the Bass staff)

(Left hand plays notes in the Treble staff)

Teacher's Note: Cross-hand work is excellent for developing *independence of the hands*. Hanon, Czerny or scales may also be played cross-hands. Many pieces can be adapted to cross-hands by playing the bass notes with the *right* hand and the treble clef notes with the *left* hand. Playing becomes more interesting and valuable finger dexterity is achieved.

Traffic Signals

Traf - fic sig - nals, traf - fic sig - nals, Here's a red light, stop!

Traf - fic sig - nals, traf - fic sig - nals, Watch the traf - fic cop.

Traf - fic sig - nals, traf - fic sig - nals, Care - ful not too fast.

Now we're get - ting close to home and here we are at last.

Finger Workout (Preparatory for pieces in G Major hand position, pages 20-21-22)

Play the line below in three ways: **1.** As written.

2. Cross-hands, with Right hand OVER the Left hand, same as "Over the Bridge," page 18.

3. Cross-hands, with Right hand UNDER the Left hand, same as "Under the Bridge," page 18.

20

G Major Hand Position

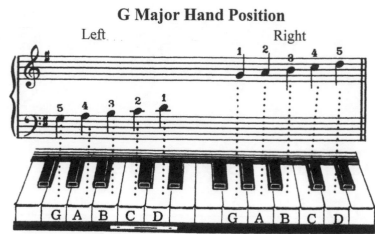

Note: Even though F# is not used in "Rowing Upstream," the sharp must appear in the *key signature* because the piece is built on the G-major *scale* (see page 27).

Rowing Upstream

There are separate dynamic marks for each staff. The melody is *f* – the accompaniment is *p*.

Rowing Downstream

This melody is the same as the piece on page 20, except that it is in the *bass* staff.

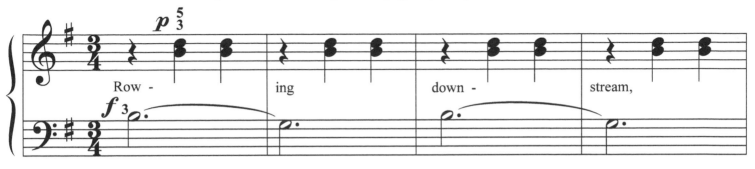

Play "Rowing Downstream" Cross-Hand Style
1. Left hand plays the treble staff accompaniment.
2. Right hand plays the bass staff melody.
The Right hand should cross *over* the Left hand.

Use the fingerings shown in the diagram below.

Right Hand: **Left Hand:**

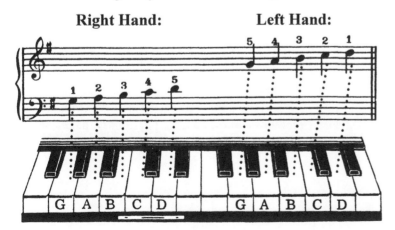

Roller Skating

Accompaniment

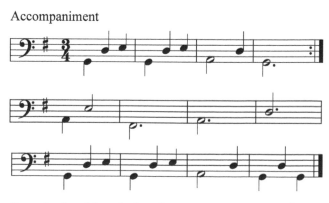

*mp is the abbreviation for *mezzo piano*, meaning medium soft (see Music Dictionary, pages 46-47).

Making Music Quiz No. 1

DIRECTIONS: Match each musical sign in the left column with the correct definition in the right column. Write the alphabetical letter of the definition on the proper dotted line. For example, number **1** (>) is an *accent*; therefore the letter **G** has been placed on the dotted line. If necessary, refer to the Reference Page (front inside cover) or the Music Dictionary (pages 46-47).

...**G**...1. >

............2. (treble clef with notes)

............3. *f*

............4. (staff with beamed notes)

............5. (staccato notes)

............6. *p*

............7. (slur)

............8. **C**

............9. ♯

............10. (treble clef with note)

............11. **3   4   2**
            4   4   4

............12. ♭

............13. (treble clef with notes)

............14. (crescendo)

............15. ♮

............16. (decrescendo)

............17. Allegretto

............18. *legato*

............19. *rit.*

............20. *mp*

A. phrase mark

B. common time   4/4

C. sharp

D. time signatures

E. medium fast

F. flat

G. accent

H. repeat sign

I. staccato notes

J. natural

K. connected

L. moderately soft

M. grow slower

N. tie

O. forte (loud)

P. third

Q. grow louder

R. piano (soft)

S. second

T. grow softer

Teacher's Note: If desired, this quiz may be given a score. Give 5 points for each correct answer.
A total score of 65 is passing – 70 is fair – 80 is good – 90 is very good – 95 or above is excellent.

Half Steps and Whole Steps

A HALF STEP is the distance from one key to the **closest** *black or white* key (there is *no key in between*). For example, F to F♯ is a half step. B to B♭ is also a half step. Sometimes a half step is from one white key to the next white key, for example B to C.

A WHOLE STEP always *skips one key*.
C to D is a whole step because there is one key in between (C♯).

Dots are used to identify different steps in the keyboard diagrams below.

H = Half Step   **W** = Whole Step

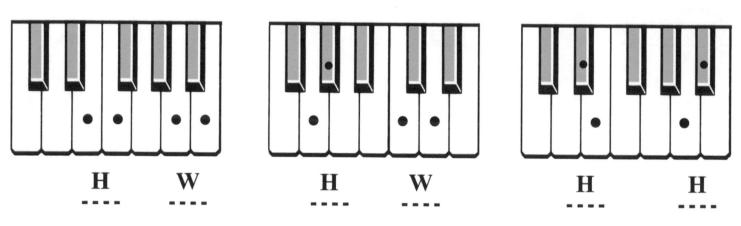

H   W   H   W   H   H

The Major Scale

A MAJOR SCALE is a pattern of whole steps and half steps in musical alphabet order.
The eight notes of a major scale have number names called *degrees*.

The keyboard below shows the **C Major scale** with degree numbers printed below each letter.
Each step is connected by a short curved line called a *slur*.
The two *half steps* are indicated with the letter H. All other steps are *whole steps*.

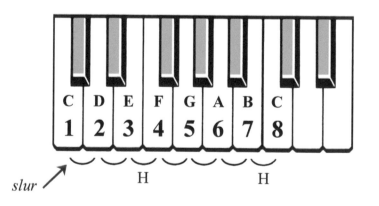

slur

C	D	E	F	G	A	B	C
1	2	3	4	5	6	7	8

H   H

• Other major scales may **start on any black or white key**.
For example, in the F Major scale, the first degree of the scale is F.

• All major scales have the **same pattern of whole steps and half steps** (same as the scale above).

• All major scales have a half step between the **3rd – 4th** degrees and between the **7th – 8th** degrees.

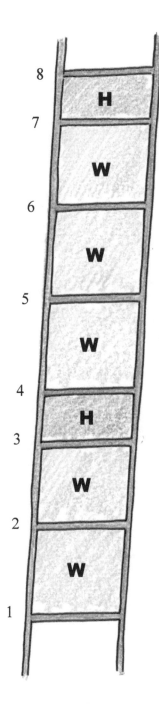

Major Scale Ladder

Notice that the eight steps of this ladder are ***unevenly spaced***. This is to show the sequence of whole steps and half steps in the major scale. The space between the 3rd and 4th steps and between the 7th and 8th steps is *smaller* because they are ***half steps***.

The numbers represent the ***degrees*** of the scale.
The letter **W** is printed between ***whole*** steps.
The letter **H** is printed between ***half*** steps.

Benefits of Scales

Playing scales involves special movement of the thumb and fingers.

    1. The thumb is ***crossed under*** the fingers.

    2. Fingers are ***crossed over*** the thumb.

Thumb and finger crossings are used frequently as music becomes more advanced. This is why it is so important to learn to play scales.

Many pieces use parts of various scales. Being familiar with the notes and fingering of scales makes learning and playing music easier.

 CORRECT FINGERING is essential in playing scales. Watch the finger numbers carefully as you play the C Major scales below.

The scales should be played ***legato***.

Thumb and finger crossings should be played as smoothly as possible, with a ***minimum of wrist movement.***

C Major Scale – Right Hand

C Major Scale – Left Hand

 The melody for this piece is based on the C major scale.
As a preparatory, play the C major scales at the bottom of page 25.

Climbing and Sliding

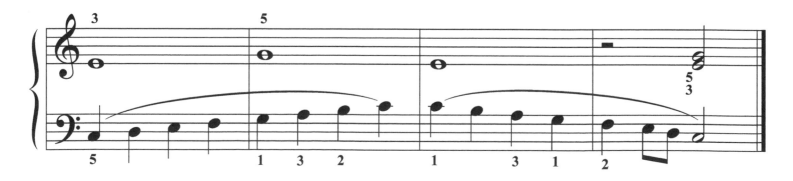

Transposing

To transpose means to play a piece in a key that is **different** from the original key of the piece.
The **melody sounds the same**, but starts on a a higher or lower note.

When transposing you use:

     1. a different **key signature**.
     2. notes from a different **scale**.
     3. different **hand positions** and **fingering**.

Below are two scales. Play the **right** hand G major scale, then play the **right** hand F major scale. Notice that they sound similar, but one is a **transposed** version of the other. Do the same for the left hand scales.

G Major Scale – Right Hand – Refer to the Front Inside Cover for any unfamiliar notes.

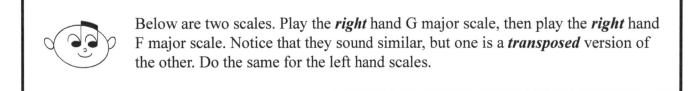

G Major Scale – Left Hand

F Major Scale – Right Hand – Refer to the Front Inside Cover for any unfamiliar notes.

F Major Scale – Left Hand

28

Finger Workout

Play this exercise five times daily as a warmup for "Tie Score."

Tie Score

Key of F Major – one flat

Score is all tied up, In this ball game.

Both teams try - ing hard, To break the tie.

Hope that it will be, Our vic - to - ry.

Cars of Long Ago

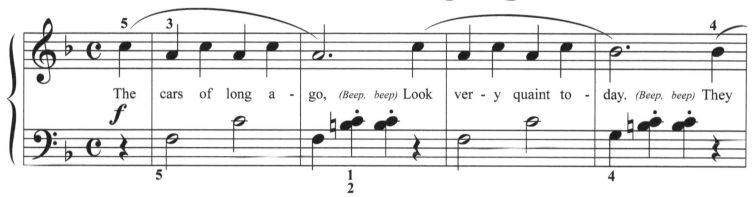

The cars of long a - go, *(Beep, beep)* Look ver - y quaint to - day. *(Beep, beep)* They

had to turn a crank, *(Beep, beep)* To start them on their way. *(Beep, beep)* They

did - n't trav - el far, *(Beep, beep)* The en - gines of - ten stalled. *(Beep, beep)* But

these old - fash - ioned cars, *(Beep, beep)* Be - gan the mo - tor age.

Accompaniment

30

 Port is a navy term for the LEFT side of a boat or ship.

Starboard indicates the RIGHT side.

This piece is to be performed in two ways:
1. Left hand ALONE –
use finger numbers *below* the bass staff.

2. Right hand ALONE –
use finger numbers *above* the treble staff.

Port and Starboard

LEFT Hand Position

RIGHT Hand Position

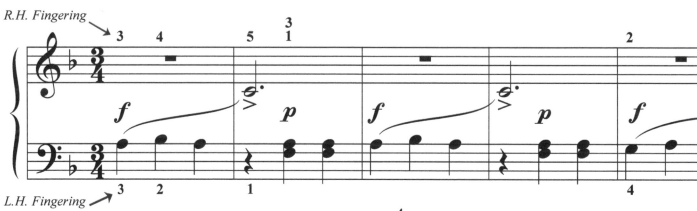

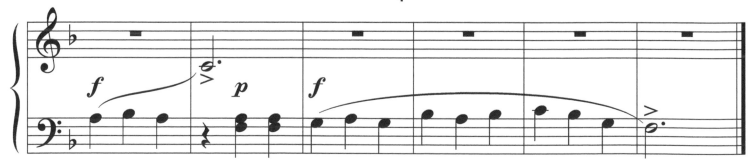

Accompaniment

Hiking Song

Bavarian Folk Song

Key of B-flat Major -
two flats

Swing a - long, with a song, As we hike thru the

woods, On a care - free sum - mer day.

We will stop, lat - er on, Eat our lunch, rest a

while. Then we'll take the home - ward trail.

Left Hand Over

Teacher's Note: The B-flat major **flash cards** may be introduced with this piece (see page 3).

State Fair

Two flats: B♭ and E♭

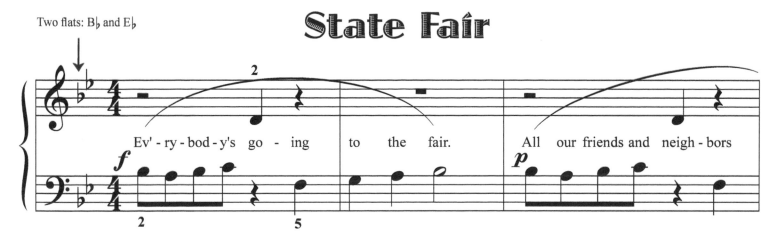

Ev' - ry - bod - y's go - ing to the fair. All our friends and neigh - bors

will be there. Farm - ers and mer - chants put on their show.

Lots of new prod - ucts we'll get to know. Fire - works will light the

sky at night. This is al - ways such a thrill - ing sight.

rit.

Rocking the Boat

This piece has a lot of *dissonance* (see page 9).

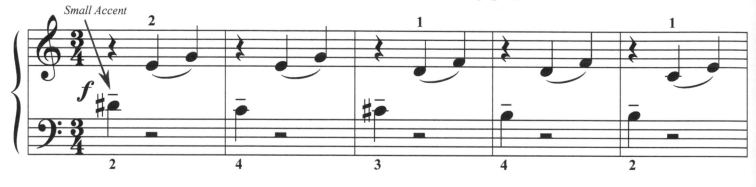

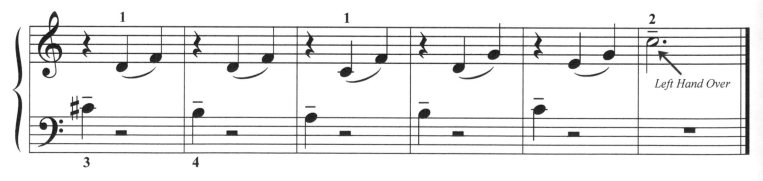

Finger Workout (Preparatory for pieces in D Major hand position, pages 35-36-37)

Play the line below in three ways. **1.** As written.

2. Cross-hands, with Right hand OVER the Left hand, same as "Over the Bridge," page 18.

3. Cross-hands, with Right hand UNDER the Left hand, same as "Under the Bridge," page 18.

Rhythm Section (Preparatory)

𝄴 ♩ 𝅗𝅥 ♩ ♩ | ♩ ♪♪ ♩ ♩ | ♩ ♪♪ ♩ ♩ | ♩ ♩ 𝅗𝅥 |

1　2　3　4　　1　2 & 3　4　　1　2 & 3　4　　1　2　3　4

Count aloud, 1 – 2 – 3 – 4, to each measure. Clap hands on each note.
This is the rhythm pattern for "The Bagpiper."

The Bagpiper

The music begins very loud and gets gradually softer as the bagpiper marches away into the distance.

The repeated whole notes in the left hand imitate the sustained low sound of bagpipes called a *drone bass.*

Key of D Major

Fortissimo (very loud)

Pianissimo (very soft)

Cross-Hand Assignment: Play "The Bagpiper" crossing the Right hand OVER the Left hand. Right hand plays notes in the **Bass** staff. Left hand plays notes in the **Treble** staff. Use hand positions shown in *Finger Workout* on page 34.

Teacher's Note: The D major *flash cards* may be started with this piece (see page 3).

MEDLEY

A *medley* is a group of two or more pieces played one after the other without pause between. For example, this piece may be combined with two others, as follows:
1. "Rowing Upstream" (page 20)
2. "Blowing Bubbles" (pages 36-37)
3. "Rowing Downstream" (page 21)

A medley is a good idea for a recital performance.

Blowing Bubbles

German Folk Song (adapted)

Two Sharps: F♯ and C♯

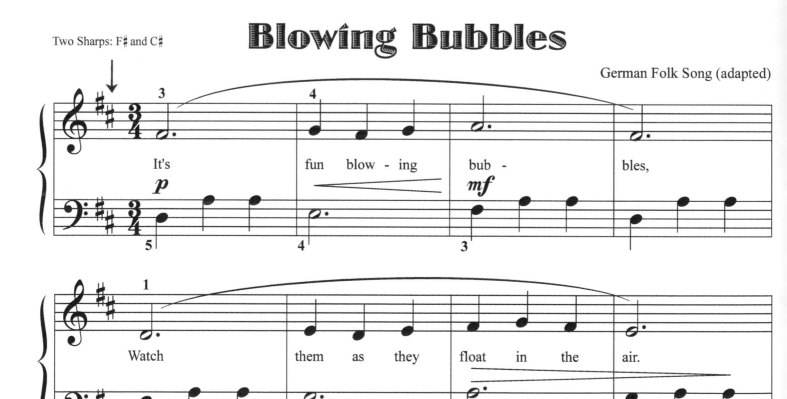

It's fun blow-ing bub- bles,

Watch them as they float in the air.

In won-der-ful col- ors,

They drift here and there. *p* Soon af - ter we

make them they burst in air. *mf* Don't wor - ry be - cause there are

lots to spare. *p* It's fun blow - ing *mf* bub -

bles, They drift here and there. *rit.*

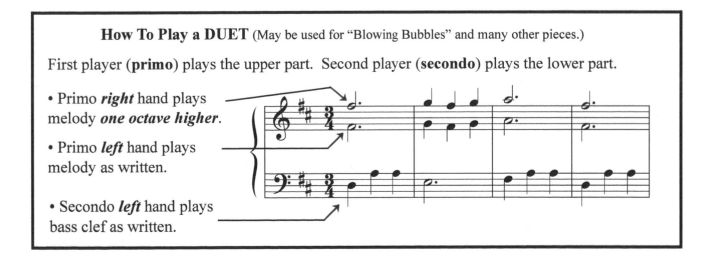

How To Play a DUET (May be used for "Blowing Bubbles" and many other pieces.)

First player (**primo**) plays the upper part. Second player (**secondo**) plays the lower part.

• Primo *right* hand plays melody *one octave higher*.

• Primo *left* hand plays melody as written.

• Secondo *left* hand plays bass clef as written.

A CHORD is a group of three or more notes that blend when played together.

Left hand chords:

Teacher's Note: The student should learn the chords by playing them. Delay the harmonic analysis until a more advanced level.

The Elephant

Key of D major

The el - e - phant's a trav - el - er, From far a - cross the

D major chord

A7 chord

seas. His cir - cus acts are fun to watch, He real - ly likes to

please. He al - so has a room - y trunk, To take where - e'er he

goes. He gets re - wards and treats ga - lore, For fun - ny tricks he knows.

fortissimo (very loud)

Cross-Hand Assignment: Play "The Elephant" crossing the Right hand OVER the Left hand. Right hand plays notes in the **bass** staff. Left hand plays notes in the **treble** staff. Use hand positions shown in *Finger Workout* on page 34.

40

Left Hand Intervals

5th   2nd   3rd

The Helicopter

Right Hand Position

Allegro *(fast)*

Frank Lynes (adapted)

Practice Suggestions:

1. Name the number of each interval in the left hand.

2. Play the treble clef notes with *both hands one octave apart,* as explained for the *primo* player on page 37.

3. Play "The Helicopter" as a duet, as described on page 37.

4. Memorize "The Helicopter" (as a solo).

Major and Minor

A melody in a major key usually sounds happy, cheerful and bright. In a minor key, the same melody sounds sad, mysterious or spooky. In this piece, the first two lines of music have a *major* sound. The last two lines have a *minor* sound.

Chimpanzee Cha Cha

D.C. al Fine means to go back to the beginning and play again, ending at the word *Fine*.
See music dictionary, page 46, for pronunciations and more explanation.

Satellites

Andante *(moderately slow)*

Sat - el - lites in space, Or - bit - ing the earth. Send - ing sig - nals

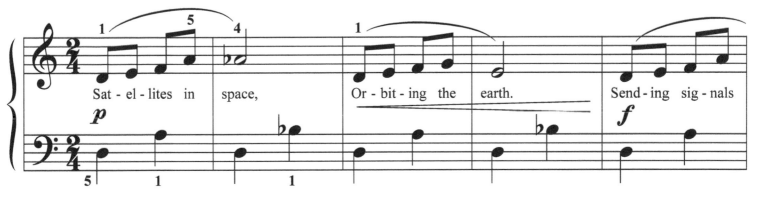

back, Bring - ing us new facts. Sat - urn and Ve - nus,

Ju - pi - ter and Nep - tune, Up in out - er space, There's a lot to learn.

Finger Workout
Look up *parallel motion* and *contrary motion* in the Music Dictionary on pages 46-47.

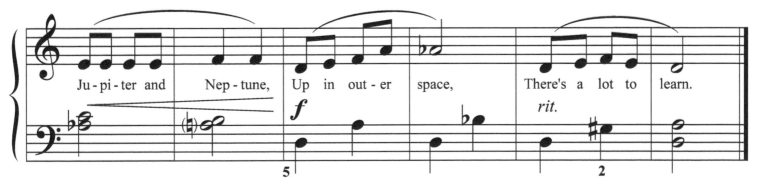

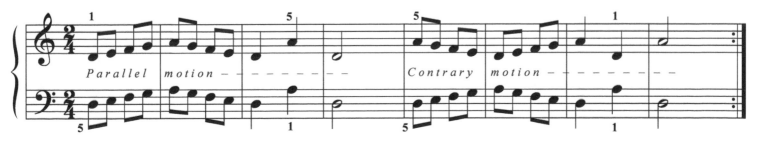

Parallel motion — — — — — — *Contrary motion — — — — — —*

Teacher's Note: This piece is in the key of D minor. However, accidentals are used instead of a key signature. At this level, the student should experience the minor sound without a technical explanation of relative major and minor.

Making Music Quiz No. 2

DIRECTIONS: Match each musical sign in the left column with the correct definition in the right column. Write the alphabetical letter of the definition on the proper dotted line. If necessary, refer to the Reference Page (front inside cover) or the Music Dictionary (pages 46-47).

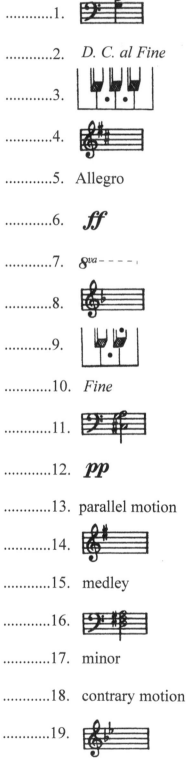

...........1.

...........2. *D. C. al Fine*

...........3.

...........4.

...........5. Allegro

...........6. *ff*

...........7. *8va* – – – –

...........8.

...........9.

...........10. *Fine*

...........11.

...........12. *pp*

...........13. parallel motion

...........14.

...........15. medley

...........16.

...........17. minor

...........18. contrary motion

...........19.

...........20. chord

A. the end

B. key of B♭ major

C. fortissimo (very loud)

D. groups of notes moving in the *same* direction

E. play one octave higher

F. sad or mysterious sound

G. key of D major

H. *Da Capo* (go back to beginning and play to *Fine*)

I. fast

J. whole step

K. key of F major

L. groups of notes moving in *opposite* directions

M. key of G major

N. group of 3 or more notes that blend when played together

O. half step

P. pianissimo (very soft)

Q. fourth

R. A7 chord

S. group of two or more pieces played one after the other

T. D major chord

Teacher's Note: If desired, this quiz may be given a score. Give 5 points for each correct answer.
A total score of 65 is passing – 70 is fair – 80 is good – 90 is very good – 95 or above is excellent.

Certificate of Progress

This certifies that

_____

has successfully completed

LEVEL ONE

of the Schaum
Making Music Method

and is eligible for advancement to
LEVEL TWO

_____

Teacher

_____

Date

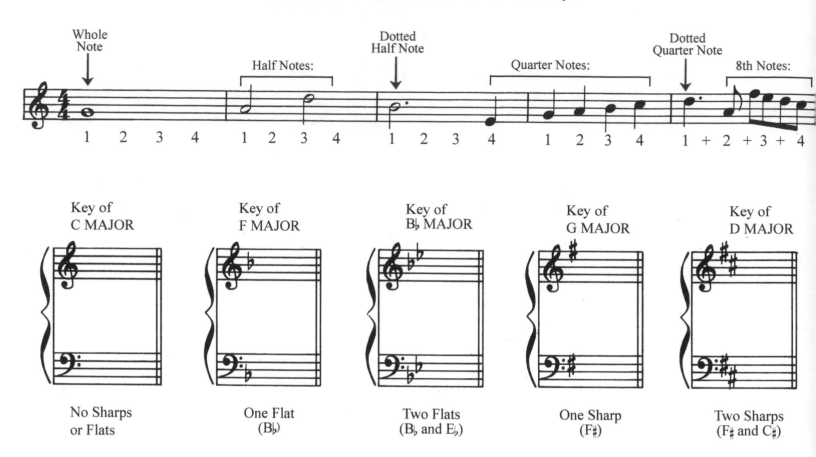

Music Dictionary

Most musical terms are Italian, because music writing began in Italy. The accented syllable is shown in capital letters.

Terms listed here are limited to those commonly found in Level One methods and supplements.

See the Reference Page (front inside cover) for illustrations of basic elements and correlation of notes with their keyboard location.

accent (ACK-sent) Stress or emphasis on a note or chord. Indicated with the symbols: — > ∧

accidental Sharp, flat or natural that does *not* appear in the key signature.

adagio (ah-DAH-jee-oh) Slow, slowly.

allegretto (ah-leh-GRET-toh) Medium fast. A little slower than *allegro*.

allegro (ah-LEG-grow) Fast, quickly.

andante (ahn-DAHN-tay) Moderately slow.

animato (ah-nee-MAH-toh) Lively, spirited.

beam Thick line connecting the stems of two or more 8th notes.

chord (KORD) Simultaneous sounding of three or more notes that blend when played together. See page 38.

common time 4/4 meter. Time signature is: 𝄵 See page 9.

con brio (kone BREE-oh) With vigor, spirit or gusto.

contrary motion Movement of notes, intervals or chords in *opposite* directions. See page 43.

cresc. Abbreviation for *crescendo*.

crescendo (cre-SHEN-doh) Gradually increasing in loudness. Also indicated with the sign: ⟨

da capo al fine (dah KAH-poh ahl FEE-nay) Return to the beginning and repeat, ending at the word *fine*. See page 42.

D.C. al fine Abbreviation for *da capo al fine*.

degree Number given to each note of a major or minor scale in ascending sequence. See page 24.

dim. Abbreviation for *diminuendo*.

diminuendo (di-min-you-END-oh) Becoming gradually softer. Also indicated with the sign: ⟩

dissonance (DISS-ah-nunse) Harsh, disagreeable sound made by two or more notes sounding together. See page 9.

duet (doo-WHET) Music for two performers. See *primo* and *secondo*. See page 37.

dynamic marks Symbols and words indicating changes of loudness. For example, *diminuendo*, *f* *p*

8va Abbreviation for *octave higher sign*.

expression marks Musical words and instructions affecting tempo, loudness and mood. For example, *allegro, misterioso,* *ff*

f Abbreviation for *forte*: loud.

fermata (ferr-MAH-tah) Hold or wait on a note or chord, longer than its normal duration. Symbol: 𝄐

ff Abbreviation for *fortissimo*: very loud.

fine (FEE-nay) End. See *da capo al fine*. See page 42.

flag Short curved line attached to the right side of a stem. A quarter note is changed to an 8th note by adding a flag.

(♭) Accidental in parenthesis used as a reminder. May also be (♯) or (♮)

forte (FOHR-tay) Loud, strong. Abbreviation: *f*

fortissimo (fohr-TISS-ee-moh) Very loud. Abbreviation: *ff*

giocoso (jee-oh-KOH-soh) Humorously, playfully.

half step The interval from one key (of keyboard) to the next closest key, black or white. See page 24.

interval Distance in sound between one note and another. See page 10.

key signature One or more sharps or flats at the beginning of each staff, next to the clef sign.

largo (LAHR-goh) Very slow, solemn.

legato (lah-GAH-toh) Notes played in a smooth and connected manner. Usually indicated with a *slur*.

leger line (LED-jer) Short horizontal line placed above or below the musical staff. Used for writing notes beyond the normal range of the staff. For example, Middle C is written on a leger line.

lento (LEN-toh) Slow, but not as slow as *largo*.

L.H. Abbreviation for *left hand*.

maestoso (my-ess-TOH-soh) Majestic, dignified, proudly.

major scale Pattern of whole steps and half steps in musical alphabetical order. See pages 24-25.

major sound Sound that is happy, cheerful and bright, based on a major scale. See page 42.

major triad Chord built using the 1st, 3rd, and 5th degrees of any major scale.

medley (MED-lee) Group of two or more pieces played one after the other without pause between. See page 36.

metronome (MET-roh-nome) Device to determine tempo or speed in music. Measured in beats per minute. The original mechanical metronome was attributed to J.N. Maelzel, therefore the abbreviation M.M. (Maelzel's metronome).

mezzo forte (MET-zoh FOHR-tay) Medium loud, softer than *forte*. Abbreviation: *mf*

mezzo piano (MET-zoh pee-YAA-noh) Medium soft, louder than *piano*. Abbreviation: *mp*

mf Abbreviation for *mezzo forte*: Medium loud.

minor Chord, melody or scale often having a sad, mysterious or spooky sound. See page 42.

misterioso (miss-teer-ee-OH-soh) Mysteriously.

M.M. Abbreviation for Maelzel's metronome. See *metronome*.

moderato (mah-dur-AH-toh) At a moderate tempo or speed.

mp Abbreviation for *mezzo piano*. Medium soft.

note head Round part of a musical note.

octave (AHK-tiv) Interval of an 8th; the top and bottom notes have the same letter name.

octave higher sign Play the notes one octave higher than written. Abbreviation: 8*va* or **8** Often used with a dotted line above the notes affected. See page 41.

p Abbreviation for *piano*: Soft.

parallel motion Movement of notes, intervals or chords in the same direction (up or down). See page 43.

phrase (FRAZE) Group of successive notes dividing a melody or accompaniment pattern into a logical section. This is similar to the way commas and periods divide a text into sections.

phrase mark Curved line (slur), placed over or under groups of notes, indicating the length of a phrase. The notes of the phrase are usually played *legato*. See page 8.

pianissimo (pee-ah-NISS-ee-moh) Very soft. Abbreviation: *pp*

piano (pee-YAA-noh) Soft. Abbreviation: *p*

pianoforte (pee-yaa-noh-FOR-tay) Original full name for the *piano*, chosen because it was the first keyboard instrument to effectively play in a wide range from very soft to very loud, thus the combination of words *piano* and *forte* (literally: soft-loud).

pp Abbreviation for *pianissimo*: Very soft.

primo (PREE-moh) First part or player. In a piano duet the first (upper) part is labeled *primo*; the second (lower) part is labeled *secondo*. See page 37.

reminder accidental A sharp, flat or natural sign in parenthesis to remind the performer to play the correct note.

repeat sign Two dots in the staff to the left of a double bar indicating that the previous section of music is to be repeated once. See page 6.

repertoire (reh-per-TWAR) Musical compositions previously studied, mastered and currently maintained by a musician or musical group so that performance can be given with a minimum of preparation.

R.H. Abbreviation for *right hand*.

rit. Abbreviation for *ritardando*.

ritard. Abbreviation for *ritardando*.

ritardando (ree-tahr-DAHN-doh) Gradually getting slower in speed.

root 1.) Key note, fundamental note, or tonic note of a chord. Lowest note of a root position chord. 2.) First degree of a scale.

scale Sequence of musical notes collectively forming a key or tonality, usually named after the starting note. See pages 24-25.

secondo (seh-KAHN-doh) Second part or player in a duet. The first part is called the *primo*. See page 37.

semplice (SEMM-plee-chay) Simple, plain.

slur Curved line, placed over or under groups of notes indicating *legato*. Often the same as a *phrase mark*.

staccato (stah-KAH-toh) Short, detached, separated. Indicated by a dot *above* or *below* a note head.

staff Group of five horizontal lines used for placement of music notes.

stem Vertical line attached to a note head.

tempo (TEMM-poh) Rate of speed used for musical beats or meter.

tempo di marcia (TEMM-poh dih MAHR-chee-ah) March time.

tempo mark Word or words at the beginning of a piece of music explaining the rate of speed to be used. For example, *allegro, andante, tempo di marcia*.

tie Curved line that connects two notes in the same staff line or space that are next to each other. The values of the tied notes are added together joining into one continuous sound. See page 5.

transpose (trans-POZE) To play a melody or chord in a key that is different from the original key, starting on a higher or lower note. When transposing you use a different key signature, notes from a different scale and a different hand position. See pages 27 and 38.

triad (TRY-add) Chord with three notes.

vivace (vee-VAH-chay) Lively, quick.

vivo (VEE-voh) Lively, animated.

whole step The distance from one key (of keyboard) to another with *one key in between*. The same as *two half steps*. See page 24.

Reference Page

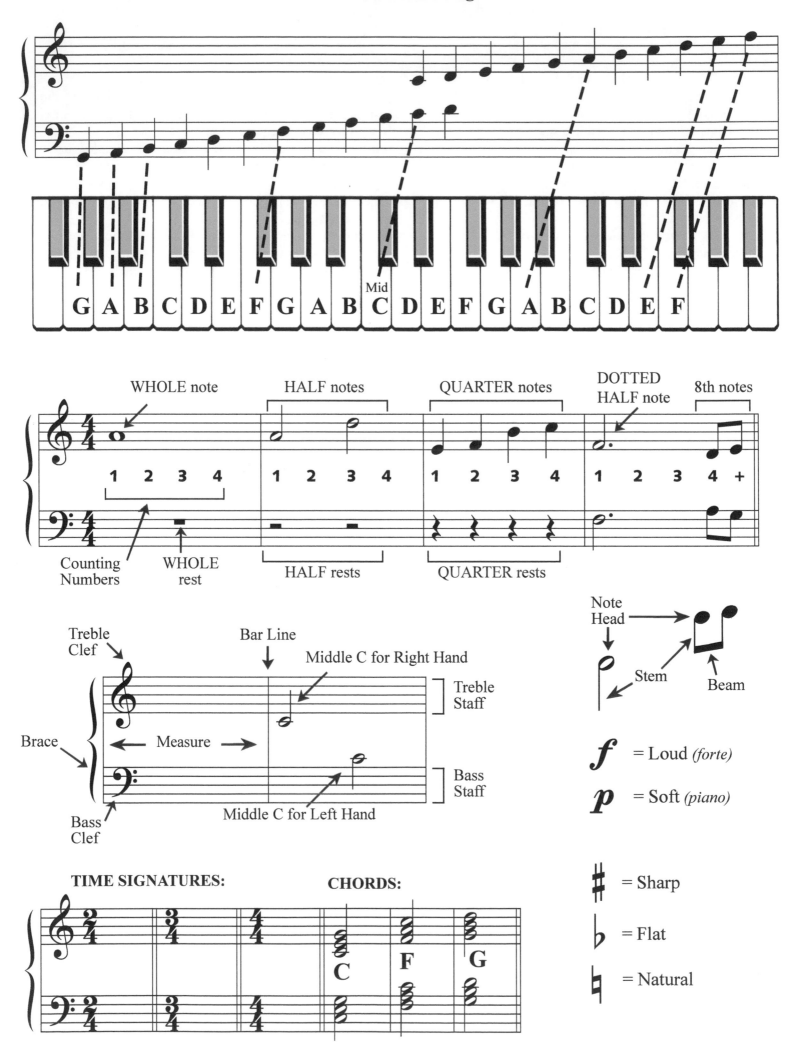